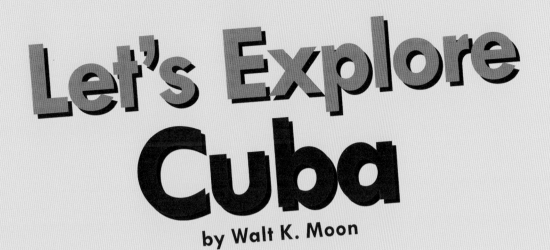

Let's Explore
Cuba

by Walt K. Moon

BUMBA BOOKS™

LERNER PUBLICATIONS ◆ MINNEAPOLIS

Note to Educators:

Throughout this book, you'll find critical thinking questions. These can be used to engage young readers in thinking critically about the topic and in using the text and photos to do so.

Lerner Publications Company
A division of Lerner Publishing Group, Inc.
241 First Avenue North
Minneapolis, MN 55401 USA

For reading levels and more information, look up this title at www.lernerbooks.com.

Library of Congress Cataloging-in-Publication Data

Names: Moon, Walt K., author.
Title: Let's explore Cuba / by Walt K. Moon.
Description: Minneapolis, MN : Lerner Publications, 2017. | Series: Bumba Books — Let's explore countries | Includes bibliographical references and index. | Audience: K to 3. | Audience: Ages 4 to 8.
Identifiers: LCCN 2016019652 (print) | LCCN 2016020021 (ebook) | ISBN 9781512430073 (lb : alk. paper) | ISBN 9781512430158 (alk. paper) | ISBN 9781512430165 (eb pdf)
Subjects: LCSH: Cuba—Juvenile literature.
Classification: LCC F1758.5 .M66 2017 (print) | LCC F1758.5 (ebook) | DDC 972.91—dc23

LC record available at https://lccn.loc.gov/2016019652

Manufactured in the United States of America
1 – VP – 12/31/16

Expand learning beyond the printed book. Download free, complementary educational resources for this book from our website, www.lernerresource.com.

Table of Contents

A Visit to Cuba

Cuba is a country

in North America.

This country is an island.

4

Cuba has flat plains.

It has hills.

The weather is warm.

Summers are rainy.

Sharks swim in the sea

near Cuba.

Colorful birds fly around.

Manatees live in rivers.

manatees

9

Cuba has many farmers.

Coffee is a major crop.

Other farmers grow fruit.

What other crops might farmers grow?

Most Cubans live in cities.

The biggest city

is Havana.

It is in the western part

of Cuba.

**How would life
in Havana be
different from
life on a farm?**

Many people visit Cuba.

They enjoy the weather.

They go to beaches.

What do you think people do at Cuba's beaches?

15

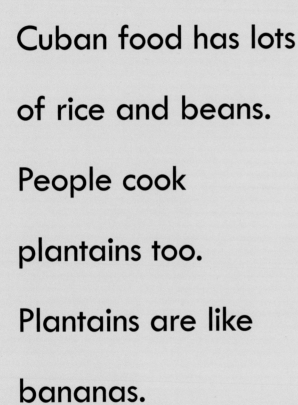

Cuban food has lots
of rice and beans.
People cook
plantains too.
Plantains are like
bananas.

plantains

16

rice and beans

Baseball is the
top sport.
Many Cubans
play baseball.
The best players
are big stars.

Cuba is a beautiful country. There are many things to see. Would you like to visit Cuba?

21

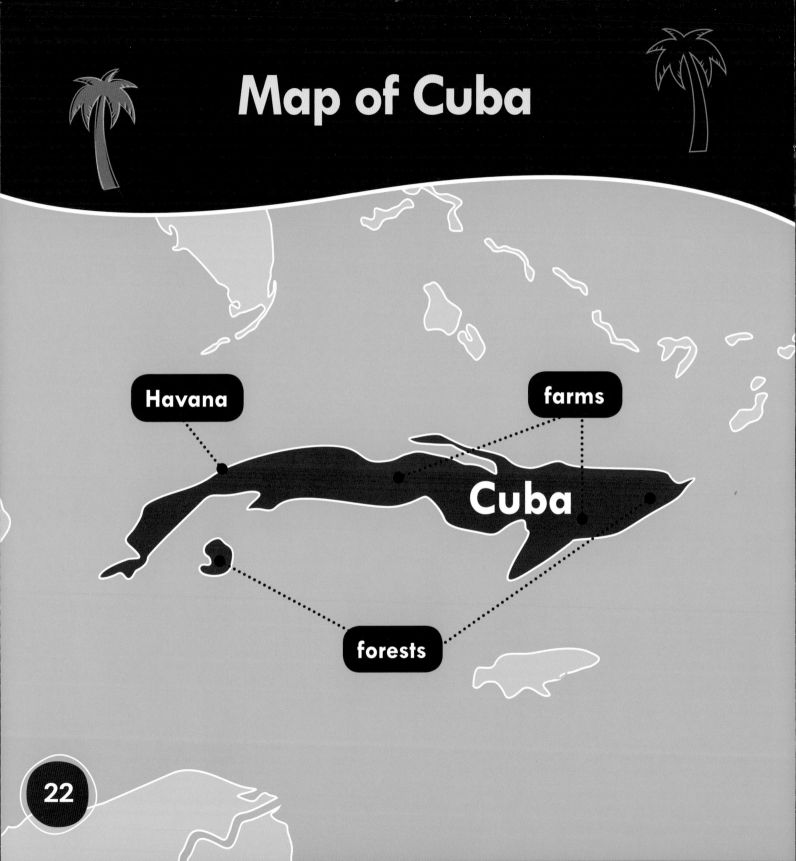

Map of Cuba

Havana

farms

Cuba

forests

Picture Glossary

crop

a plant grown for food or goods

island

a piece of land surrounded by water on all sides

manatees

large animals that have flippers and live in the water

plantains

fruit like bananas that people cook and eat

23

Index

Read More

Cantor, Rachel Anne. *Cuba.* New York: Bearport Publishing, 2016.

Cavallo, Anna. *Cuba.* Minneapolis: Lerner Publications, 2011.

Flynn, Brendan. *Baseball Time!* Minneapolis: Lerner Publications, 2016.

Photo Credits

The images in this book are used with the permission of: © Dmitry Chulov/iStock.com, p. 5;
© Tupungato/Shutterstock.com, pp. 6–7; © Greg Amptman/Shutterstock.com, pp. 9, 23 (bottom left);
© Sabino Parente/Shutterstock.com, pp. 10–11, 23 (top left); © Hang Dinh/Shutterstock.com, pp. 12–13;
© Kamira/Shutterstock.com, p. 14; © Lisa F. Young/Shutterstock.com, pp. 16–17, 23 (bottom right);
© Conde/Dreamstime.com, pp. 18–19; © Anna Jedynak/Shutterstock.com, pp. 20–21; © Red Line
Editorial, p. 22; © energizzzer/Shutterstock.com, p. 23 (top right).

Front Cover: © Nobohh/Dreamstime.com.